Edition Schott

Alvin Singleton
b.1940

Jasper Drag

for violin, clarinet, and piano
für violine, klarinette und klavier

ED30053

Full Score

www.schott-music.com

Mainz · London · Madrid · New York · Paris · Prague · Tokyo · Toronto
© 2000 SCHOTT MUSIC CORPORATION, New York · Printed in USA

First Performance
November 12, 2000
The Phillips Collection, Washington, D.C.

Verdehr Trio
Elsa Ludewig-Verdehr, clarinet
Walter Verdehr, violin
Silvia Roederer, piano

Duration: ca. 9'

Foreword

Jasper Drag was commissioned by Michigan State University and the Phillips Collection for the Verdehr Trio. The work is scored for clarinet, piano, and violin. The title refers to the June 7, 1998 Jasper, Texas incident, wherein three white men dragged a black man to his death after chaining him to the back of a pickup truck. The composer writes, "This composition is not intended to tell a story, or even to evoke images. *Jasper Drag* is meant to be a marker on the collective memory of a nation still growing. The score is inscribed to the memory of James Byrd, Jr., the victim of this racially motivated act."

Carman Moore
2000

Einleitung

Das für Klarinette, Klavier und Geige geschriebene Stück *Jasper Drag* wurde von der Michigan State Universität und dem Phillips Collection Kunstmuseum für das Verdehr Trio in Auftrag gegeben. Der Titel weist auf das Vorfall am 7. Juni 1998 in Jasper, Texas hin, wobei drei weiße Männer einen schwarzen Mann ans Heck ihres Pick-Ups ketteten und ihn zu Tode schleiften. Der Komponist schreibt, "Der Zweck dieses Kompositions ist weder Geschichtenerzählen noch bildiche Darstellung. *Jasper Drag* soll als ein Merkzeichen im kollektiven Gedächtnis einer immer noch erwachsenden Völkerschaft dienen. Das Werk ist dem Andenken von James Byrd Jr., der Opfer dieser rassistisch motivierten Tat, gewidmet.

Carmen Moore
2000

übersetzt von Celia Barry

Commissioned by Michigan State University and
The Phillips Collection for the Verdehr Trio

JASPER DRAG

In memory of James Byrd Jr.

Alvin Singleton (2000)

ED30053

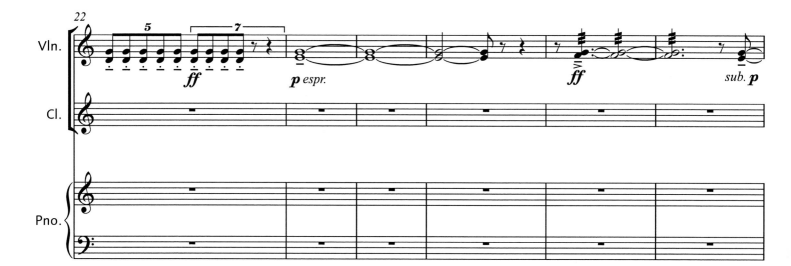

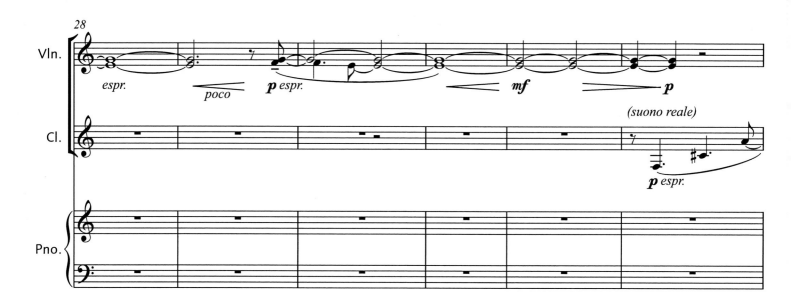

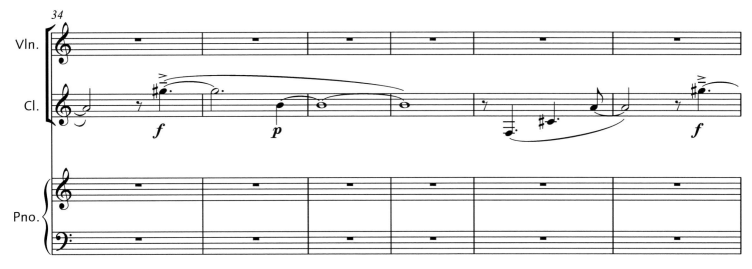

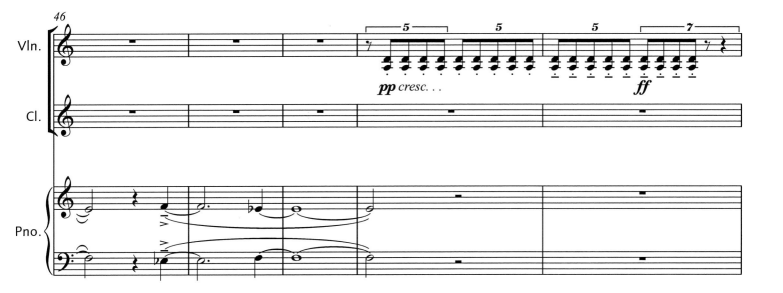

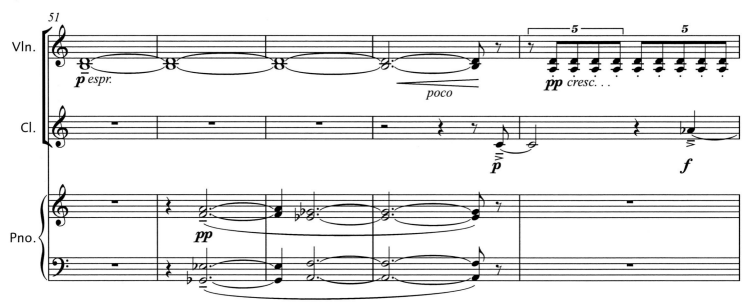

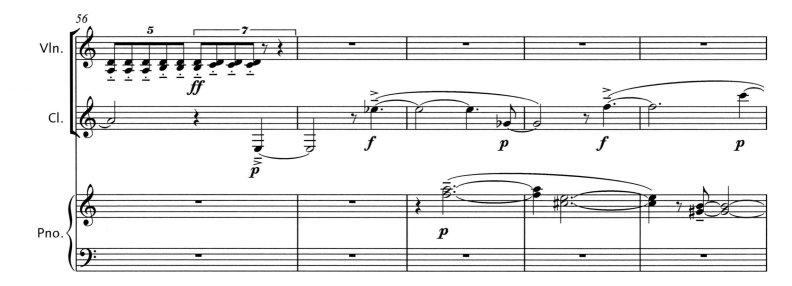

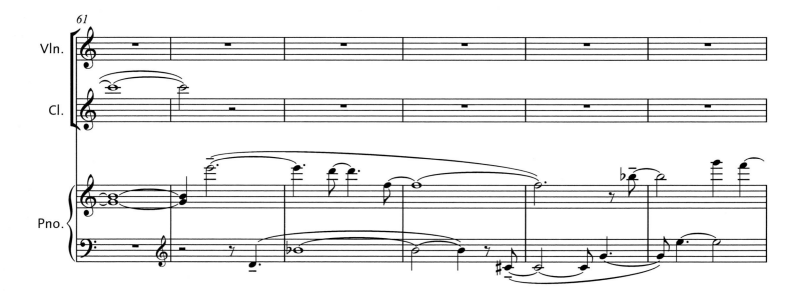

Clarinet in B♭

Commissioned by Michigan State University and
The Phillips Collection for the Verdehr Trio

JASPER DRAG
In memory of James Byrd Jr.

Alvin Singleton (2000)

Clarinet in B♭

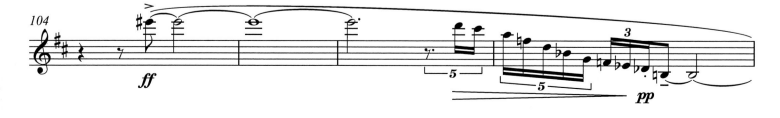

Violin

Commissioned by Michigan State University and
The Phillips Collection for the Verdehr Trio

JASPER DRAG
In memory of James Byrd Jr.

Alvin Singleton (2000)

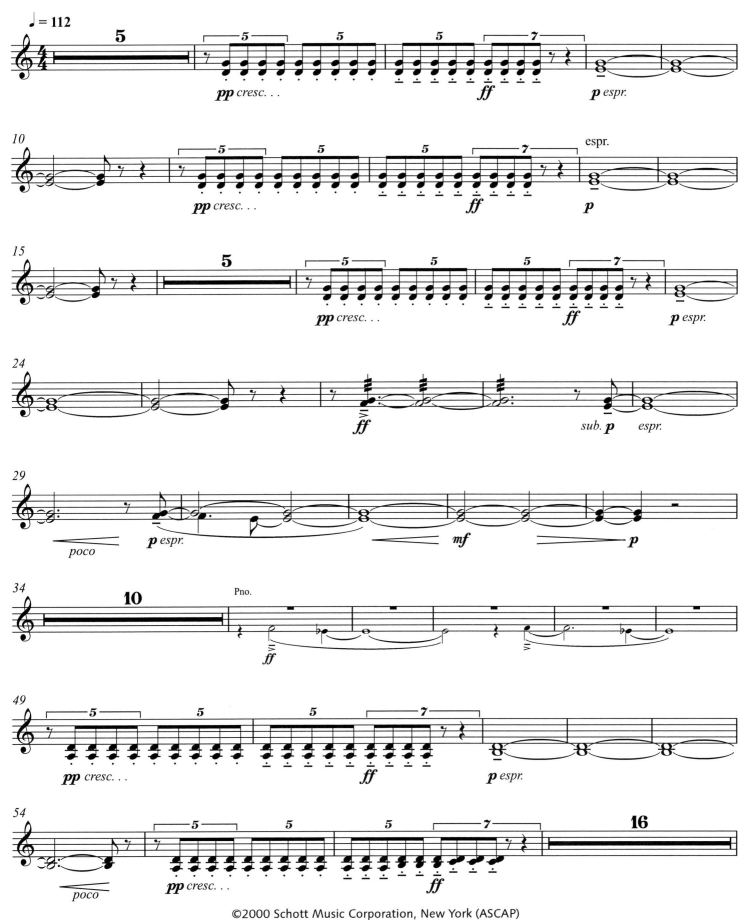

Violin

tenuto non espr.

Piano

Commissioned by Michigan State University and
The Phillips Collection for the Verdehr Trio

JASPER DRAG

In memory of James Byrd Jr.

Alvin Singleton (2000)

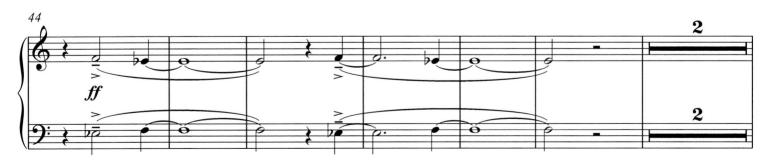

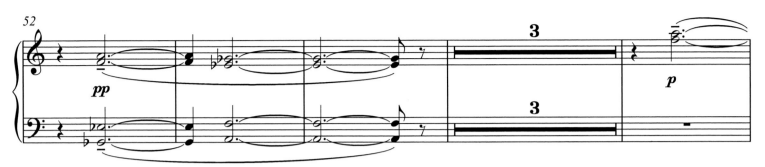

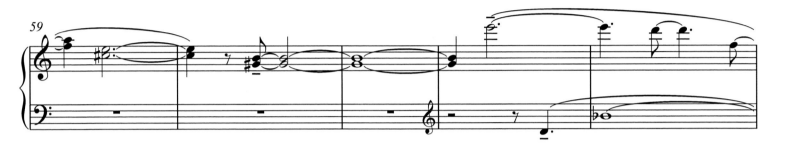

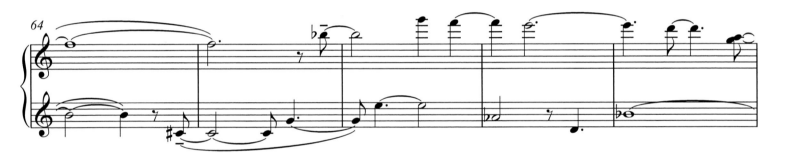

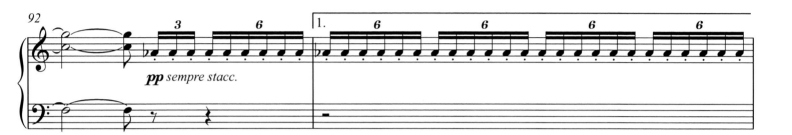

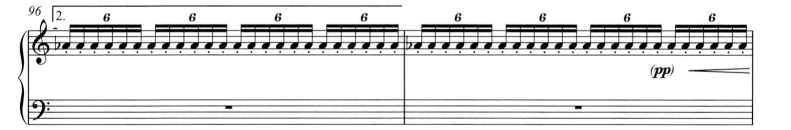

Piano

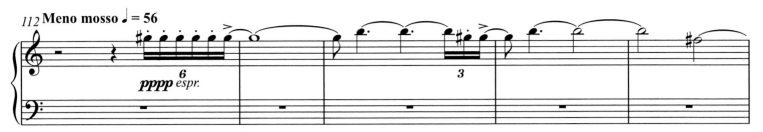

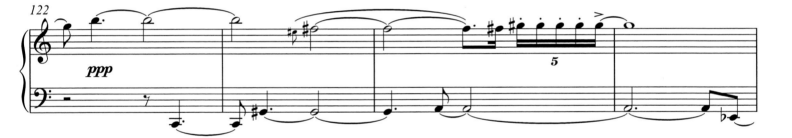

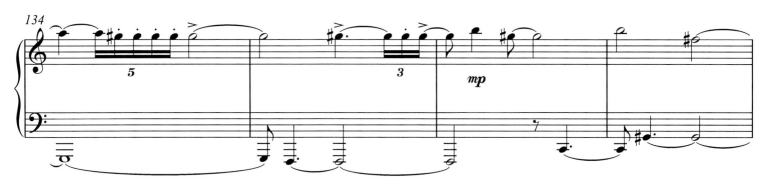

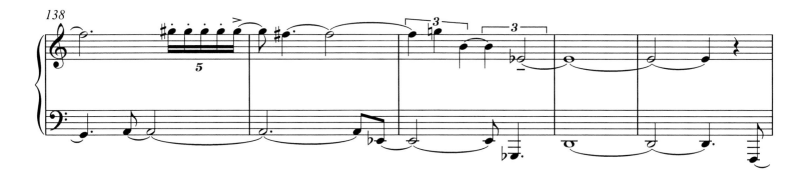

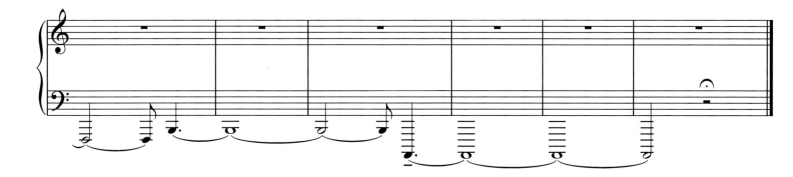

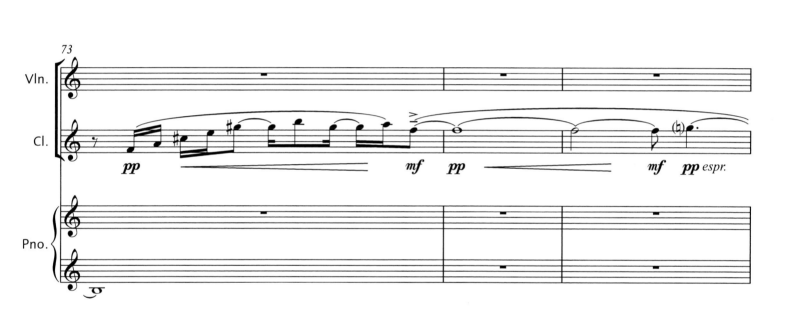

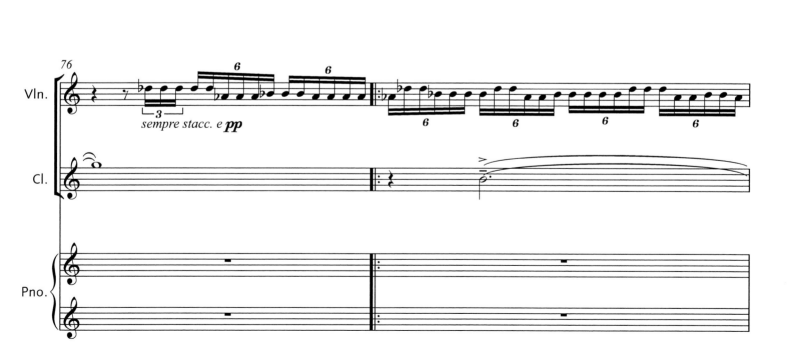

6

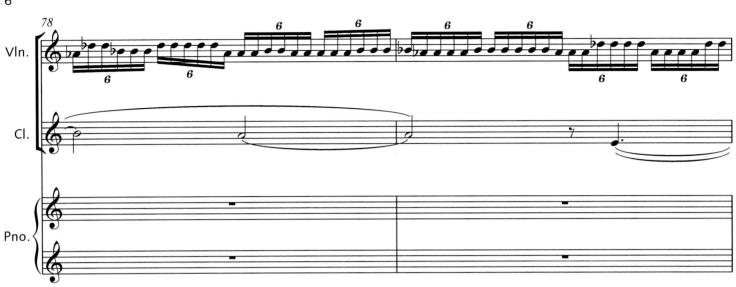

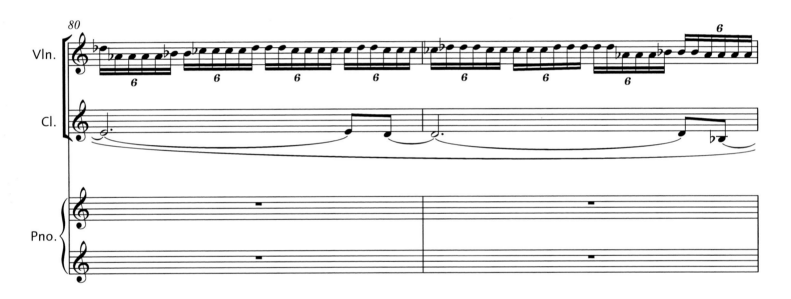

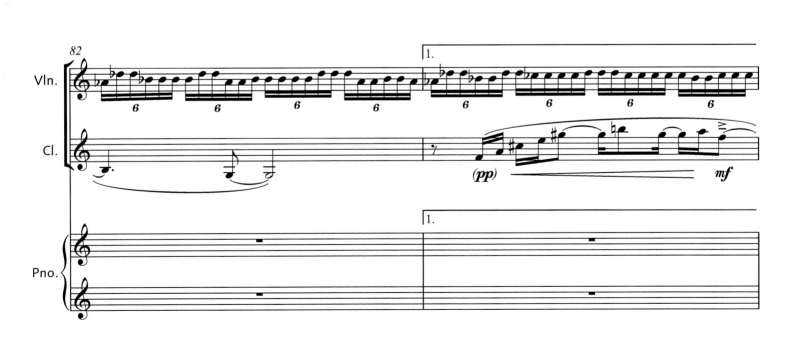

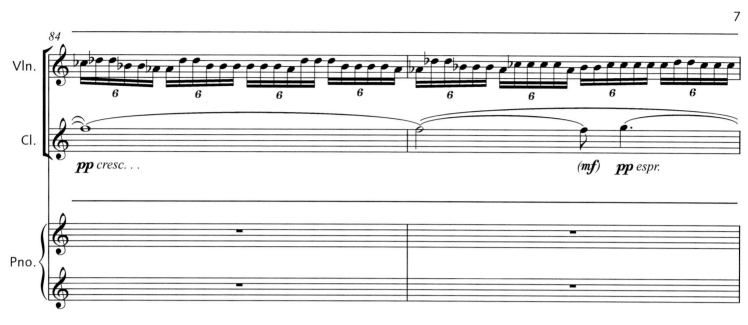

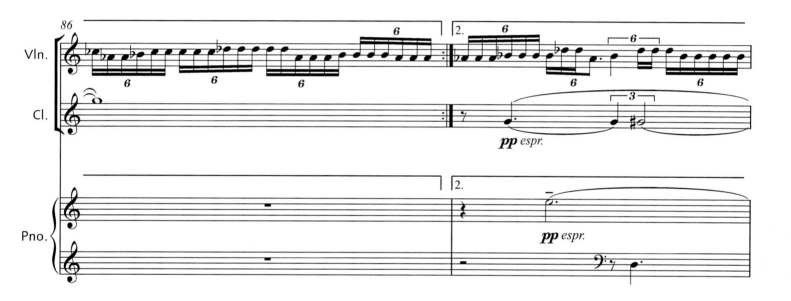

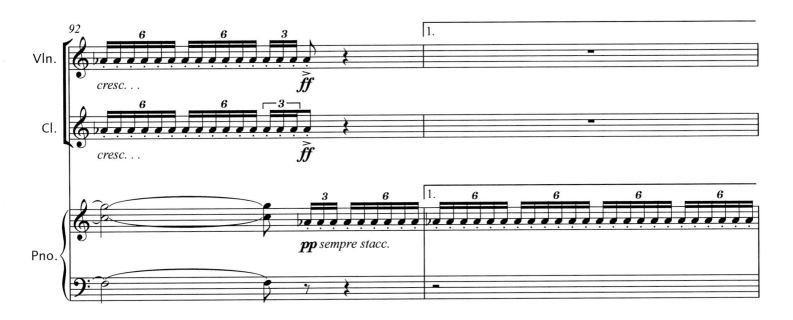

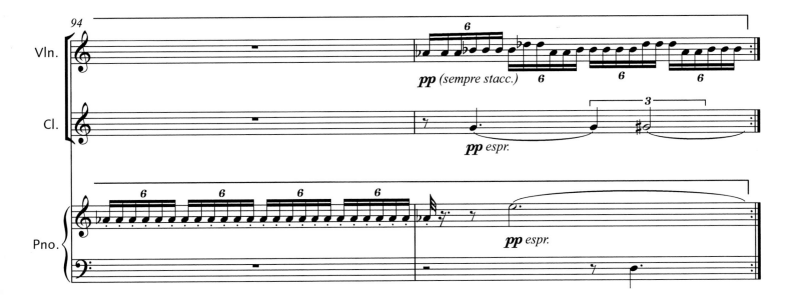

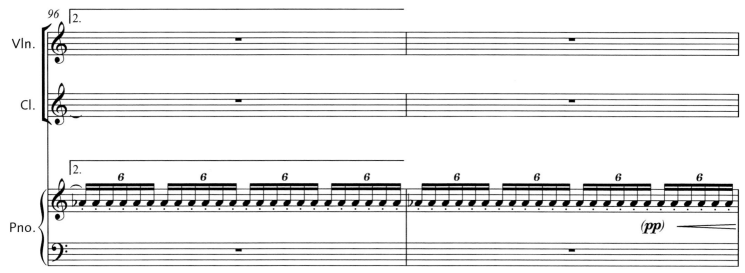

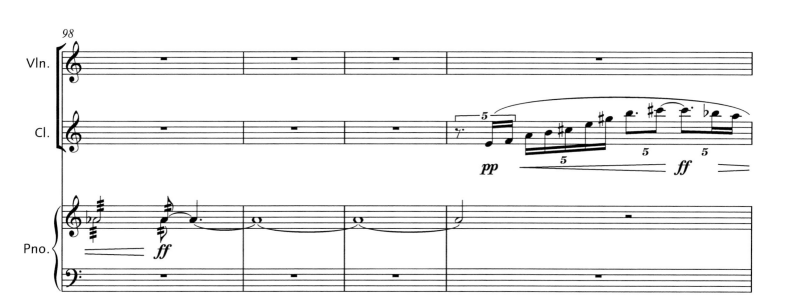

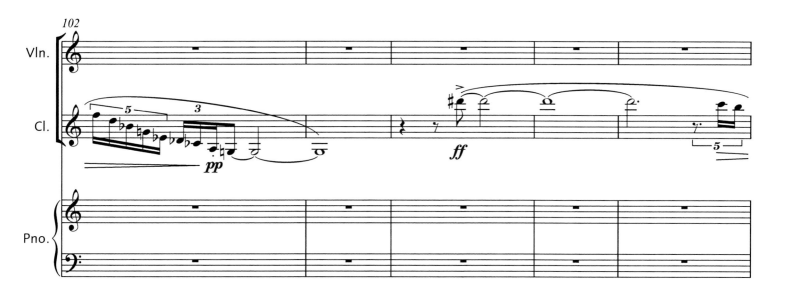

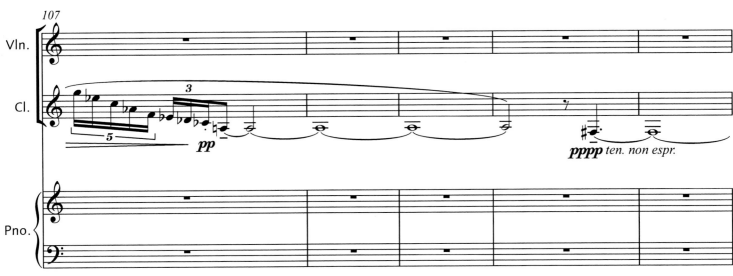

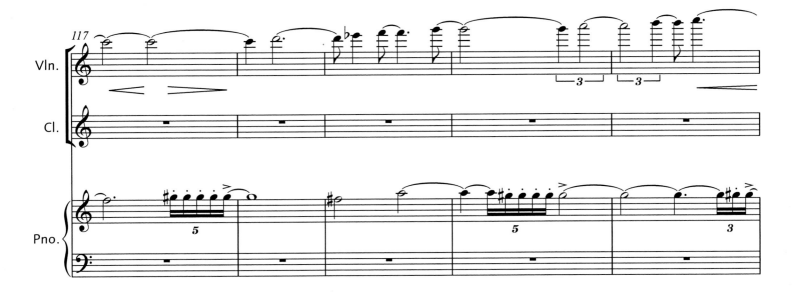

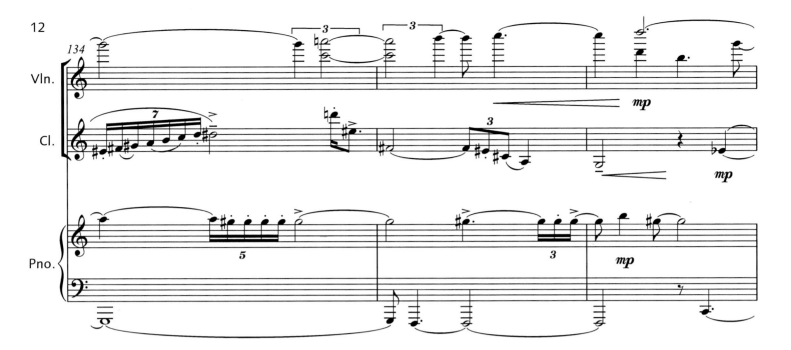

4 September 2000
Civitella Ranieri Center
Umbertide, Italy